Table of Contents

16 Ways to Change Your Life

Susan Kersley

While every precaution has been taken in the preparation of this book, the publisher assumes no responsibility for errors or omissions, or for damages resulting from the use of the information contained herein.

16 Ways to Change Your Life

Table of Contents

Introduction

Teachers open the door. You enter by yourself Chinese proverb

If you are someone who wants to change, remember that the power is in your hands.

The best way to initiate what you want is for **you** to do something different. Until you do, your life will continue as before.

You have to take action, for things to change.

When you do things differently, others change their response to you. When something changes, everything else shifts too – just like a spreadsheet.

I offer you **16 strategies**: Apply them and you will live the life you truly want. Even if you only follow some of the suggestions your life will change. Don't delay.

Here are the 16 Ways to change your life:

1. Communicate effectively
2. Develop better relationships
3. Manage your time
4. Look after yourself
5. Set and achieve your goals
6. Be supported
7. Improve your work-life balance
8. Have fun and be happy
9. Get involved in your community
10. Be in touch with your spirituality
11. Increase your abundance
12. Discover your life's purpose

13. Find your beliefs and values
14. Increase your skills
15. Change one thing
16. Do what you must do

You will notice there is an overlap between many of the strategies for change. Don't be overwhelmed by the number of ideas I offer you. If you follow just one strategy you will find you are well on your way to achieving many of the others. This is because 'life is like a spreadsheet - change one thing and everything else changes.'

Start today, because without action on your part, your life will continue the way it always has.

You can do it.

1. Communicate effectively.

When you are about to change the way you do something you may need to explain to others around you why you are about to behave differently.

If you make a dramatic change by stopping something you've been doing for ages, or starting something new, tell others because they may wonder what has happened to you.

It's important to improve the way you communicate with people who may be affected by your change in behaviour.

Too many people don't get as far as talking about what they would like to do because they assume that others would be upset or not approve. That might be true but you won't know their reaction until you take action. By communicating your intentions, you help to prepare others for what you will do.

Effective communication is an essential skill that can improve your personal and professional relationships. Whether you're engaging in a conversation, delivering a message, or creating written content, the following strategies can help you communicate clearly.

Get into rapport with the other person. This means finding a connection with them so that they really hear what you are telling them. This can involve:

Speaking to them at a time when they can give you their full attention.

- make sure they are listening to you.
- be on the same physical level as them (both of you sitting, or both of you standing)

If you think they may not like what you say, start with something positive, then tell them about what is going to happen, and finish with how your change will be a win-win for both you and them.

If people don't seem to hear or understand what you say: listen twice as much as you speak. You have two ears and one mouth!

Understand their point of view because when you show understanding they are more likely to give you the attention and consideration you want. State your message clearly and concisely. Avoid using jargon or complex language that may be confusing.

Listen actively by paying attention to what the other person is saying and let them ask questions if necessary. Show you are listening by nodding and making eye contact.

Respect boundaries by being aware of their personal space and avoid interrupting or talking over them. Respect their opinions and views, even if they differ from your own.

Be patient if communication is breaking down, take a step back and try approaching the situation again from a different angle.

Know your audience and understand their needs by adapting your message based on who you are speaking to. Consider their interests, background, and knowledge level.

Adjust your tone by using a tone that resonates with your audience. Be formal in professional settings, and more casual when appropriate.

Be clear and concise by organising your thoughts

by structuring your ideas logically. Use bullet points or numbered lists when possible.

Avoid jargon by using simple language to prevent confusion. If technical terms are necessary, be prepared to explain them.

Listen actively by engaging fully by paying attention to the speaker without planning your response while they are talking.

Show understanding by nodding and paraphrasing what the other person has said to confirm what you've heard.

Use body language by maintaining eye contact, using gestures, and an open posture. Ensure your expressions match your message to avoid mixed signals.

Ask questions if something is unclear, ask open-ended questions to gain more insight.

Encourage dialogue by inviting others to share their thoughts and opinions.

Be aware of the feelings of others and respond appropriately. Acknowledge others' feelings to encourage trust and openness.

Practice assertiveness by expressing your thoughts, feelings, and needs clearly while respecting others' viewpoints.

Set boundaries by explaining your limits and preferences confidently, without being aggressive.

Provide constructive feedback, addressing specific actions instead of attacking the person.

Choose the right method to communicate by deciding between face-to-face, phone, or digital communication.

Be aware of your tone when writing as your tone may be misinterpreted, so choose your words carefully in emails and texts.

Be aware of your emotions by understanding your emotional state and how it affects your communication.

Control your responses by remaining calm and thoughtful, especially in challenging conversations.

Summarise major points after discussions by recapping important details to ensure mutual understanding.

Clarify the next steps if any actions need to be taken. Communicate them clearly to avoid confusion.

Effective communication is a skill that improves with practice. By applying these strategies and being mindful of your interactions, you'll enhance not only your ability to convey messages but also your relationships with others.

2. Develop better relationships.

Building and maintaining healthy relationships takes effort, understanding, and communication. Here are some practical tips to enhance your relationships, whether with family, friends, or romantic partners.

'Mirroring and matching' are skills you do automatically when you get on with someone. Inter-personal skills depend on being able to get into rapport with the other person. If you are unable to communicate then rapport may be missing.

For improved relationships, work on improving your rapport skills. Mirror the other person's body posture in a subtle way. Match their breathing rate and their tone of voice. Notice the type of language they use and their predominant representational language. Are they mainly visual, auditory or kinaesthetic?

Notice the words they use, then use the same type of language in reply. If they use mainly visual words then reply using the same and asking, 'Do you see what I mean?' Mainly auditory people use words such as 'I hear what you say.' Kinaesthetic people use emotional language such as 'I feel it inside me, and I know what I have to do.'

Be interested in the other person by trying to understand their world and their point of view, especially during disagreements. Imagine what it might be like if you could 'get into their shoes' and see how you might seem from their eyes. This is the ability to see their perspective and understand their feelings. By showing empathy, you can deepen your understanding of others and build stronger bonds.

Create a safe space for open discussion without criticism.

Active listening is one of the essential aspects of building a better relationship. Pay attention to what the other person is saying and refrain from interrupting. When communicating with others, it's important to show genuine interest in them and their experiences.

Build trust because it forms the foundation of every healthy relationship. To build trust, you need to demonstrate that you are reliable, consistent and honest. Follow through on your commitments and be transparent in your communication.

Be positive because positive interactions can make a world of difference in your relationships. Use positive language, be encouraging, and show appreciation for the other person.

Respect boundaries of others. This is vital to building stronger relationships. Understand and respect other people's point of view, even if it does not align with yours.

Stay open to feedback. This is key to building better relationships. Be receptive to constructive criticism and make efforts to improve accordingly.

Developing better relationships takes time, effort and patience. By applying these tips, you can build stronger relationships and enrich your life in the process. Share your thoughts and feelings honestly. Being open about what matters to you encourages trust. Listen to understand, not just to respond but to show empathy and confirm the other person's feelings.

Regularly express gratitude for what the other person does. A simple 'thank you' can go a long way.

Be there to celebrate both small and big victories.

Spend quality time together. Find mutual interests and spend time doing things you both enjoy. Put away distractions like phones and devices to focus on each other.

Be supportive by being there during tough times. Your support can strengthen your bond. Support each other's goals and dreams Be reliable and follow through on commitments. This builds trust. Honesty is crucial. Share your thoughts and feelings truthfully.

Talk about your boundaries clearly. Respect each other's space and privacy. Understand that it's okay to have different views and that variety can enrich a relationship. When conflicts arise, tackle them head-on but calmly. Avoid escalating tensions. Focus on finding a solution rather than placing blame.

Let go of resentments. Holding onto past hurts can damage relationships. Practice forgiveness to move forward. Reflect on what went wrong and try to improve, rather than dwelling on negative experiences.

Regularly assess your own behaviour and influence on the relationship. Be willing to learn and change. Sometimes, talking to a mental health professional can provide valuable insights into your relationships.

Improving relationships is an ongoing process that requires commitment and effort from all involved. By practicing open communication, empathy, and authenticity, you can deepen your connections with those around you. Strong relationships contribute significantly to your overall well-being and happiness. Start today and watch your relationships thrive!

3. Manage your time.

If you don't have time to do the things you really like to do, decide what you could stop. How many tasks could be outsourced or delegated? Are there more efficient ways to do those tasks?

Time management is a vital skill that can increase productivity, reduce stress, and improve overall quality of life. Here are some practical strategies to help you make the most of your time.

Plan to do important things first. Don't leave them until the last minute. Notice which of your urgent tasks could either be delegated or could have been planned and done on a regular basis over a period. Identify the most important tasks for the day and make sure to complete them first. Keep a to-do list and schedule tasks according to their level of importance.

Become aware of your time wasters and cut down or stop them. Recognise what commonly distracts you, social media, emails, noisy environments, and reduce these. Create a dedicated area for work or study that is free from interruptions. Keeping your workspace organised can prevent distractions and help you find what you need quickly.

Create a plan. Set aside specific times for tasks and stick to them. This will help you manage your time more efficiently. Turn off notifications on your electronic devices and close the door if you need a quiet space to work. Avoid multitasking, as it can disrupt your focus and slow down your progress.

Take breaks. It's important to step away from work periodically to recharge your batteries. Take short breaks to clear your mind and get some fresh air.

Ask for help. Don't be afraid to ask for help when you need it. Delegating tasks can free up valuable time and make the workload more manageable.

Learn to say no. Saying yes to every request can lead to overwhelm and lack of focus. Learn to say no when you need to manage your time.

Set SMART goals. These are specific, measurable, achievable, relevant, and timed. Identify which goals are most important and urgent. Focus on those that align with your values and objectives. Set clear goals: short-term versus long-term goals. Define what you want to achieve both soon and in the future.

Plan ahead. Use a planner or digital calendar to map out your days and weeks. This allows you to visualise deadlines, appointments, and priorities. Allocate specific time slots for tasks and stick to this as closely as possible to stay on track.

Group tasks as follows:

1. Urgent and important

2. Important but not urgent

3. Urgent but not important

4. Neither urgent nor important

Spend more time on tasks that contribute to your long-term goals and less on those that are merely urgent.

Break jobs into smaller steps. Large projects can be overwhelming. Divide them into smaller, manageable tasks.

Use the Pomodoro technique. Work for 25 minutes, then take a 5-minute break. After four cycles, take a longer break. This can help maintain focus and prevent burnout. Use tools and technology to organise tasks and deadlines and to set reminders and keep track of important dates.

Spend time each week reviewing what you accomplish, what didn't get done, and why and adjust accordingly. Life can be unpredictable. Be prepared to adjust your plans when necessary.

Effective time management is a vital skill that requires discipline and effort. By managing your time you can be more productive, reduce stress, and achieve better work-life balance.

4. Look after yourself.

Self-care is an essential part of living a healthy and balanced life. It is important to dedicate time to yourself to recharge and rejuvenate your body and mind. Do not neglect your own needs. It's important to care for your body, mind and spirit.

You can achieve this by moving regularly, eating healthily, keeping your brain active by learning, reading and enquiring, and your spirit by connecting with your inner self, Higher Being, or God, according to your own beliefs. Music, creativity or yoga can connect with all of these.

When you make big changes in your life you need to have energy. Make sure you eat and exercise regularly and healthily. Keep your brain active by lifelong learning and remaining interested in the world around you whatever your age.

Start your day with mindfulness - a few moments of mindfulness meditation. Sit in a comfortable position, close your eyes, take a few deep breaths, and focus on your thoughts, sensations, and feelings. Notice your thoughts, without judgment, and let them go. Do this for a few minutes each morning and notice how it sets a peaceful tone for the day.

Take care of your body by exercising regularly and eating nutritious foods. Make a plan that suits your lifestyle and stick to it.

Make time for relaxation for reducing stress and anxiety. Take a relaxing bath or enjoy some quiet time reading a book. Disconnect from all screens and enjoy some peace.

Connect with nature by spending time outside. This helps to refresh your mind and body. Take a walk outside to ground yourself.

Create a restful environment and develop a bedtime routine to signal your body that it's time to wind down Finish by reflecting on the good things that happened during the day, even the smallest ones. This can be a great way to shift your focus from things that are worrying you, to the things that bring you happiness and joy.

Sleep well by getting 7-9 hours of quality sleep each night. This is essential for good health and leaves you refreshed for the day ahead.

Create a daily or weekly self-care plan that includes activities you enjoy.

Prioritise physical health. Aim for at least 30 minutes of exercise most days of the week. Find activities you enjoy, such as dancing, hiking, or yoga.

Eat nutritious foods. Focus on a balanced diet rich in fruits, vegetables, whole grains, and proteins. Consider preparing meals in advance to save time and promote healthy eating.

Stay hydrated by drinking plenty of water throughout the day to keep your body functioning optimally.

Limit screen time. Take breaks from digital devices to improve your mental clarity and focus on real-life interactions.

Improve emotional wellness by journalling. Write down your thoughts and feelings to process emotions and reflect on your experiences.

Seek support by connecting with friends, family, or a therapist if you're feeling overwhelmed. Sharing your thoughts can provide relief and perspective.

Connect with your creativity by exploring interests such as painting, gardening, writing, or playing a musical instrument. Taking part in creative activities can boost your mood and provide a sense of accomplishment. Learn something new by taking a course or attending workshops to stimulate your mind and for personal growth.

Set boundaries. Learn to say no to commitments that drain your energy or time. Put your well-being first over unnecessary obligations. Have some time and space for yourself without distractions.

Foster healthy relationships by surrounding yourself with positive people. Build a support network of friends and family who uplift and inspire you. Express your needs and feelings.

Limit negative influences. Identify and minimise interactions with people or situations that drain your energy or bring negativity into your life.

Adjust your self-care routine regularly. Evaluate what is working and what isn't. Be flexible and willing to alter your approach as your needs change.

Celebrate your achievements. Acknowledge your progress and treat yourself kindly for the efforts you put into your self-care.

Improving your self-care requires a willingness to put yourself first. By bringing these ideas into your daily life, you can improve your overall well-being and be a healthier, happier you. Self-care is not selfish, it's essential. By taking time out for yourself, you can feel refreshed, rejuvenated and energised.

5. Set and achieve your goals.

Setting and achieving goals requires dedication, flexibility, and a willingness to change. You can improve your chances of success leading to a more fulfilling life. The journey towards your goals is just as important as the destination. Stay committed, keep learning, and enjoy the process!

Imagine being projected into your future life when you've achieved what you want and look back as you are now. Tell the present 'you' what to do differently to enable you to achieve what you want. Setting and achieving goals is important for personal success.

Decide what you want instead of what you don't want. Set specific goals and a time frame by when to achieve them.

The first step in achieving your goals is to define them. Clearly state what you want to achieve. Instead of saying 'I want to get fit,' say 'I want to run a 5K in under 30 minutes.' Make a list of your goals and prioritise them. Writing your goals makes them more tangible and reinforces your commitment.

Imagine achieving your goal. This positive vision can motivate you to work towards it. Tell friends, family, or colleagues about your goals. This creates a support system and increases accountability.

Create a plan, for achieving what you want. Break big goals down into smaller, achievable steps, and decide deadlines to achieve them. Outline the specific steps you need to take to reach each milestone. This could include daily, weekly, or monthly tasks. This makes the overall goal less overwhelming and helps track progress. Decide by when you want to achieve your goal. This creates urgency and helps select your actions.

Staying motivated is key to achieving your goals. Find a way such as tracking your progress, rewarding yourself for achieving milestones, or seeking support from others. Put in the effort and make the necessary changes to move closer to your goals. Don't be afraid to take risks or make mistakes, as these can be valuable learning opportunities.

Review your goals and action plan, if something isn't working, don't hesitate to adjust your approach. Learn from setbacks. If you encounter challenges, view them as learning experiences rather than failures. Analyse what went wrong, adjust your strategy, and keep moving forward.

Celebrate success and recognise what you accomplish. This reinforces your motivation and reminds you of the progress you've made. Sometimes, goals need to be modified based on changes in circumstances or personal growth. It's okay to adapt as you progress. Once you achieve your goal, take time to reflect on the journey. What worked? What didn't?

6. Be supported.

Everyone needs support at different times in their life. It's especially important to find the most suitable person or group to help you at a time of change.

Your mentor, or coach is ideally someone not too much involved in your life so that you are able to talk quite openly and not feel judged. They should accept what you tell them without criticism. In that way you can bounce ideas on them and discover what you need to do.

Who or what supports you? Are you supported by family, friends, colleagues, coach, mentor, group, books, radio or TV programmes? Support is best when it enables you to make your own decisions.

If you're struggling in any way with stress, anxiety, relationship issues, or anything else, there are resources available. Whether that means talking to a trusted friend or family member, seeking help from a therapist or counsellor, or a support group.

Don't be afraid to take the first step in seeking help. Asking for support is a sign of strength, not weakness. You deserve to feel happy, healthy, and fulfilled, and there is no shame in searching for what helps you achieve those things.

The right support, emotional, professional, or educational, can significantly influence your well-being and success.

Reflect on what's happening and consider what type of support you would like. Is it emotional support, professional guidance, or help with a specific project? Decide what you hope to achieve by seeking support because clear objectives will help you communicate your needs effectively.

- **Emotional support**: Friends, family, therapists, or support groups.
- **Professional support**: Mentors, career coaches, or industry experts.
- **Educational support**: Tutors, study groups, or online resources.

- **Personal network**: Talk to friends and family. Those closest to you can offer the best support and understanding.
- **Social media and online communities**: Facebook, Reddit, or specialised forums can connect you with others who share your challenges.
- **Support groups**: Look for local organisations that provide support for specific issues such as mental health, bereavement, or addiction.
- **Community Centres**: These may offer workshops, classes, or resources for various needs.
- **Professional services**: Therapists and counsellors, if you're seeking emotional support.
- **Career coaches and mentors**: Contact professionals in your field who provide insight and guidance.

- **Ask for recommendations** from trusted friends or colleagues, for their opinions or experiences with specific support resources.
- **Assess compatibility**. The right support will connect and resonate with you. Arrange an initial meeting to judge if it feels like a good fit.
- **Trial period.** Consider starting with a few sessions or meetings to decide if you're comfortable with the arrangement.
- **Engage and communicate** to build relationships. Be open and honest. Clearly express your needs, concerns, and goals with the person providing support.

- **Establish boundaries,** to ensure that the support remains beneficial for both parties.
- **Provide feedback.** Share what is working for you and what isn't, to adapt the support to your needs.
- **Adjust as needed.** Don't hesitate to seek new support if your initial choice isn't meeting your expectations.

Utilise additional tools and resources:

- Consider using mental health apps, personal development platforms, or online learning resources.

- For immediate emotional support, hotlines can help at any time.
- Participate in workshops or courses related to your area of interest to further network and gain new knowledge.

Evaluate your progress to assess whether the support you're receiving is helping you meet your goals. Life changes, and so do your needs for support. Be open to finding new resources or adjusting your current support network.

Celebrate achievements. Recognise your progress, no matter how small, and adapt your support strategy as needed.

Finding the right support takes time and effort, but the benefits are well worth it. By clearly identifying your needs, exploring resources, and maintaining open communication, you can build a support system that enhances your journey, whether in personal growth, career development, or any other area of life. Seeking help is a sign of strength and an important step towards achieving your goals.

7. Get your work and life more balanced.

If your work is your life and you have no time for anything else, then something must change. Of course, work is important and may take up many of your waking hours. Don't neglect the rest. It is vital to find time not only for your friends and family, your partner and your community also. But most vital of all is time for you, for finding out who you are when you are not in your professional role.

Finding a balance between work and personal life is essential for long-term physical, mental, and emotional well-being.

What does that mean to you? Which areas of your life do you neglect?

What steps do you need to make a difference, to make time for a life, apart from work? Allocate time in for you and treat it as important as a meeting or work commitment.

Achieving a balanced life, where work and personal time coexist well, is essential.

Make a to-do list and prioritise your tasks based on their importance and urgency. Focus on completing the most important things first and remember to take regular breaks. Create a plan that works for you and stick to it. Be sure to include time for work, personal time, and social time.

Learn to say "no" to work or social commitments that interfere with your personal time. Disconnect from your work when you are not at work. Don't let email notifications or phone calls take over your personal time.

Find a hobby or some activity that allows you to recharge and have fun in your personal time.

Practice self-care and make time to exercise, meditate, or relax. Taking care of your physical and mental health is essential to achieving balance in your life.

State your work hours by defining specific start and end times for your workday. Communicate these boundaries to colleagues and family.

Create a dedicated workspace, if working from home. Set up a space solely for work to mentally separate it from personal time.

Focus on the 20% of tasks that produce 80% of results. This helps to reduce stress.

Take advantage of variable working arrangements to better balance your timetable with personal commitments. Set limits around technology and communication during personal time. This means turning off work notifications and resisting checking emails.

Include regular physical activity into your routine, whether it's a gym session, yoga, or daily walks.

Practice mindfulness by engaging in activities that promote mental well-being, such as meditation, journalling, or spending time in nature.

Make time for loved ones. Don't neglect quality time with family and friends. Plan regular meals or outings to strengthen these connections.

Strengthen workplace relationships by networking and collaboration. This can lead to a more supportive environment, making it easier to share workloads.

Reflect on your work-life balance from time to time. If you are you feeling overwhelmed, adjust your boundaries and commitments as needed. Circumstances change, be prepared to adapt your plans to maintain balance. Consider coaching or counselling if you struggle with work life balance.

Creating a balanced life requires effort, and flexibility. By setting boundaries, prioritising personal time, and actively looking after yourself, you can develop a fulfilling life where work and personal responsibilities coexist. Balance is not a one-size-fits-all approach, it's about finding what works for you and being willing to adjust along the way.

8. Have fun and be happy.

As you go about your day, remember to have fun and be happy. Find joy in the simple things and don't take anything for granted. Make the most of every moment because life is short and unpredictable Dance in the rain, laugh with friends, and embrace new experiences. Fill your life with positivity and love and let go of anything that weighs you down.

Spend time with family and friends to share enjoyable experiences. Social interactions can boost your mood and provide support.

Take a moment each day to reflect on what you're thankful for. Keeping a gratitude journal can help you focus on positive aspects of your life, improving how happy you are.

Physical activity releases endorphins, which enhance your mood. Whether it's dancing, hiking, or practicing yoga, find a form of exercise you enjoy.

Spend time outdoors. Nature has a calming effect and can lift your spirits. Go for a walk in the park, have a picnic, or simply sit outside and enjoy the fresh air. Practice mindfulness or meditation to help reduce stress and lead to a greater appreciation for life. While technology can be fun, excessive screen time can lead to feelings of isolation and stress. Aim to have more real-life interactions and experiences.

Laughter is a universal language of happiness. Watch comedies, read funny books, or spend time with people who make you smile. Don't take life too seriously; find joy in the little things. Surround yourself with positivity. Decorate your space with items that make you smile and inspire creativity. Play uplifting music and fill your surroundings with joyful elements.

Achieve small, manageable goals to deliver a sense of accomplishment. Celebrate your successes, no matter how minor they may seem.

Helping others can enhance your own happiness. Volunteer or assist someone in need. Acts of kindness create a sense of connection and fulfillment.

Allow for spontaneity in your life. Engage in unexpected adventures or activities. Sometimes the best memories come from unplanned moments.

Treat yourself with kindness. It's okay not to be perfect and give yourself permission to feel and express your emotions.

Discover what excites you. Try new hobbies, visit museums, attend workshops, or join clubs. Engaging in activities you love to ignite passion and joy.

Challenge yourself to learn a new skill. The thrill of mastering something can bring a sense of achievement and happiness. Don't be afraid to express your individuality and pursue what you love, even if it's not mainstream.

Ensure you get enough sleep and set aside time for relaxation. A well-rested mind and body contribute significantly to overall happiness.

Happiness is a journey, not a destination. Focus on enjoying the process and allow yourself to experience joy in both big and small ways. It is not something that can be found outside of you. It's a state of mind that you create from within yourself. Focus on the positive, and let negativity have no power over you. Increase your enjoyment of life by thinking about times that were fun and happy. Bring those remembered emotions into the present and notice how you enjoy the situation much more.

As you go through life, keep these words in mind: **have fun and be happy**. They might sound simple, but they're a vital key to a fulfilling life

9. Get involved in your community.

Being involved in your community can be a rewarding way to make a positive impact and connect with others. Become involved in some way, however small. Take part in local activities. Don't take things for granted. If something would be better changed then offer to do what is necessary. This can be one of the most fulfilling things you can do. It allows you to connect with others, make a difference in people's lives, and even learn new things about yourself.

Which communities are you part of? Family, neighbours, friends, religious groups, creative groups, learning together, holidays, common activities. Many communities have clubs based on hobbies or interests (e.g. book clubs, hiking groups, or community gardening). Joining these groups can provide a sense of belonging and offer networking opportunities.

Volunteer at local charities, schools, hospitals, or community organisations. You can help in many ways, from sorting donations to tutoring students.

Attend and participate in local events such as festivals, fairs, or town hall meetings. This helps you meet people and learn more about what your community may need. Look for events at libraries, schools, or religious institutions that host volunteer opportunities and community gatherings. Check your community's calendar for festivals, concerts, and other events that bring people together. Attending these is a great way to meet new people and learn about local customs and traditions. Shop at small businesses in your community. By supporting these you are helping to create jobs and contributing to the local economy.

Attend town hall meetings to learn about the issues facing your community and how you can get involved. You may even be inspired to run for office yourself.

Discover local opportunities by looking for community organisations, or groups that support your interests. Check local government or community centres that have listings of upcoming events. Identify your interests by thinking what you're passionate about. This could be anything from environmental issues, education, health care, the arts, or social justice. Contact organisations to see how you can contribute. Many rely on volunteers for a variety of tasks, including administrative work, events, and direct service. Consider committing to a regular volunteer position, which can help deepen your connection to the community.

Campaign for change if you're passionate about a particular issue. This could include attending town meetings, writing letters to local representatives, or starting a petition. Take part in discussions that focus on local policies and issues to raise awareness.

Consider mentoring youth or tutoring students who may need extra help, if you have expertise in a particular area. Local schools or community centres often welcome volunteer tutors. Gather a group of like-minded people to collaborate on the project. Continue to build relationships with the people you meet. Networking can open more community opportunities. Stay informed about ongoing projects, volunteer opportunities, and community needs by subscribing to newsletters or joining community social media groups.

Involvement in your community can take many forms, and even small actions can make a significant difference. The key is to be proactive, open-minded, and willing to connect with others who share your passion for making a positive impact. Getting involved in your community takes time and effort, but the benefits are numerous. You'll gain a sense of belonging, make new friends, and make a positive impact on the world around you.

10. Get in touch with your spirituality.

Connecting with your spirituality is a process that requires openness, self-reflection, and a willingness to explore your inner self. Whether you profess to a religion, and this is a formal following or a background of being part of a religious group, there will be a sense of the spiritual in your life. This may show by the feeling of awe when you are in nature, see a beautiful sunrise, or a magnificent sunset, hear the ocean waves crashing on the rocks, or be inspired by the beautiful colours of the sea.

The cycles of nature and the seasons can be inspiring and make you aware of something bigger than the self alone. Getting in touch with your spirituality can be a deeply personal and enriching journey.

It's vital to nurture your spirit as much as your body and mind. If you think that spirituality is missing from your life, connect by taking time to sit and connect to your breathing. As you breathe in and out, slowly count to five during the in breath and five during the out breath. Breathing exercises help to anchor you in the present and reduce stress.

Meditation and mindfulness can quieten the mind and allow you to connect with your inner self. Set aside a few minutes each day to focus on your breath and your thoughts. Try various forms of meditation, mindfulness, guided imagery, or transcendental meditation to find what resonates with you. **Incorporate mindfulness into your daily life.** Focus on being present in the moment during everyday activities, which can deepen your sense of connection to yourself and the universe.

Expressing gratitude is a powerful way to connect with your spirituality. Take a moment each day to reflect on what you are thankful for, and express your gratitude to the universe, a higher power, or simply to yourself.

Spending time in nature can help you feel more grounded and connected to something greater than yourself. Take a walk in the woods, sit by a stream or lake, or simply spend time outside in your garden or a nearby park, observing and contemplating the world around you. Being in a natural setting can foster a deeper connection to the universe.

Take time each day to reflect on your thoughts and feelings. Write your thoughts, feelings, beliefs, and experiences. This can help clarify what spirituality means to you. Create some quiet time in your day for self-reflection, whether it's a few minutes or longer.

Seek out like-minded people because surrounding yourself with others who share your spiritual beliefs and practices can help you feel more connected and supported. Having conversations about their spiritual journeys can provide new insights and inspiration.

Engage in prayer, whether structured or spontaneous, to connect with a higher power or your inner self.

Explore books or teachings from various spiritual traditions that inspire you. Look for authors who resonate with your beliefs or who offer new perspectives. Listen to spiritual leaders and thinkers through podcasts or recorded talks, allowing their insights to inform you.

Establish small daily rituals, such as lighting a candle, saying affirmations, or engaging in gratitude practices that provide a sense of sacredness. Observe significant moments, such as solstices or personal milestones, with rituals that honour these transitions.

Explore art and creativity like painting, music, or writing to express your spirituality. This can be a powerful way to connect with your feelings and beliefs. Participate in creativity-focused workshops. These can help you tap into deeper aspects of yourself.

Listen to your intuition. Pay attention to your instincts and feelings. They can guide you and help you make decisions that resonate with your true self. Keep a dream journal and explore your dreams for deeper insights into your subconscious thoughts and feelings.

Consider finding a spiritual mentor or teacher to guide you. Professionals can help you explore your spirituality while also addressing any emotional or psychological factors that may arise. Allow yourself the space to grow and evolve over time. Be open to the mysteries of life and spirituality. Sometimes, the most profound insights come when you least expect them. Everyone's spiritual journey is unique, so take the time to explore what resonates most with you. Be gentle with yourself as you embark on this path of discovery.

There is no "right" way to connect with your spirituality. It is deeply personal and requires patience, openness, and a willingness to explore your inner world. Trust your intuition and be kind to yourself as you embark on self-discovery.

11. Increase your abundance.

Abundance is not just about material wealth, it's a mindset that encompasses various aspects of life, including health, happiness, and relationships. There are effective ways to encourage a more abundant life so you can move from scarcity to abundance, from poverty to wealth. You may need to change your beliefs and attitude towards money by valuing yourself, and how others value what you do, by paying and charging appropriately.

Focus on the abundance already in your life. This can be your health, your relationships, your job, or anything else that brings you joy and fulfillment.

Set clear intentions. When you picture yourself having more abundance, you are more likely to bring it into your life. Make a vision board or write down your goals and intentions to help you focus on them each day.

Take action towards your goals. Once you have set your objectives, it is important to take small steps every day towards your goals and celebrate your progress along the way.

Practice mindfulness and gratitude. This helps you stay present and appreciate the abundance around you. This can include meditation, journalling, or simply taking a few deep breaths to ground yourself in the present moment. Regularly take time to reflect on what you're thankful for. This helps to rewire your brain to focus on abundance rather than scarcity.

Surround yourself with people, places, and things that remind you of abundance. This can include spending time with positive and supportive friends, immersing yourself in nature, or decorating your home with items that bring you joy. Positive relationships can significantly contribute to your sense of abundance. Learn from those who embody the abundant life you aspire to achieve.

Get rid of limiting beliefs or shortage mindset that may be holding you back. Trust that abundance is available to you and that you deserve to have it in your life. Use positive affirmations to reinforce an abundant mindset. Phrases like "I am worthy of all good things" can help shift your perspective.

Define abundance and what it means to you. Set specific, measurable, achievable, relevant, and timed (SMART) goals related to your personal vision of abundance. Spend a few minutes each day imagining the abundance you seek. This can create a powerful connection between your goals and your subconscious mind. Divide your goals into actionable steps. Small consistent actions can lead to significant results over time.

Stay open to opportunities. Be receptive to new ideas and opportunities that come your way. Sometimes, abundance arrives in unexpected forms.

Invest in yourself. Dedicate time to acquiring new skills or knowledge that can enhance your life, whether through online courses, workshops, or reading.

Health and well-being. Prioritise your physical and mental health. A well-balanced diet, regular exercise, and mindfulness practices can boost your energy and overall abundance.

Practice generosity by sharing your time, money, or expertise. Generosity creates a flow of energy that can attract more abundance into your life.

Volunteer by taking part in community activities. Doing this will enrich your life and improve connections, helping you gain a broader view on abundance.

Practice meditation or mindfulness exercises to become more aware of your thoughts and feelings regarding abundance.

Reduce exposure to negativity from news, social media, or pessimistic individuals. Focus on uplifting and empowering content instead.

Regularly celebrate your achievements, no matter how small. This reinforces your belief in the abundance you are creating. Keep a journal to document your journey toward abundance, noting your successes and lessons learned.

Increasing your abundance encompasses mindset shifts, goal setting, and community building. By applying these, you will create a more fulfilling and abundant life. Abundance begins within, so nurture your mindset and watch your external reality transform.

12. Know your life purpose.

Have you ever discovered your life purpose? It is your sense of self and knowing why you are here. Finding your life purpose is important at whatever stage of life you are. By identifying your purpose, you will gain clarity about what you are doing and why. You can manage change in your life so much better once you are clear about your life purpose. Identifying your life purpose is a step beyond goal setting.

Once you are clear about your life purpose your goals became clearer because they are the steps you need to take to move towards your purpose

Knowing yourself and your life purpose can bring immense clarity, direction, and meaning to your life. It is a journey of self-discovery that requires a willingness to explore your innermost thoughts, beliefs, values, and strengths. To begin this journey, start by asking yourself some fundamental questions about your life, such as:

- What motivates me?

- What are my core values?

- What am I passionate about?

- What are my strengths and weaknesses?

- What do I want to achieve in life?

- What legacy do I want to leave?

- What impact do I want to make on the world?

Reflect on these questions and try to answer them honestly. You may discover some surprising insights about yourself that will help you understand your life's purpose. Once you have a clear understanding of yourself, it's time to explore your life further.

Life purpose is a deeply personal and individual concept. It's a unique expression of your values, passions, talents, and aspirations. Your life purpose is not something you can discover overnight. It takes time, effort, and self-reflection to uncover your purpose. Here are some steps you can take:

Listen to your inner voice. Pay attention to what excites and motivates you. Your inner voice will guide you towards your life purpose.

Identify your values. These are the principles that define you. They give you a sense of meaning and purpose.

Follow your passions. Do what you love and love what you do. Your passions reflect your purpose.

Use your strengths. These are the skills and talents that make you unique. Use them to make a difference in the world.

Look for your calling. This the work that you were meant to do. It's the contribution you make to the world.

Finding your life purpose can be a deeply personal and transformative journey. Here's a guide to help you uncover your life purpose.

Self-reflection by journalling. Spend time each day or week writing about your thoughts, feelings, and experiences. Reflect on moments when you felt most fulfilled or content.

Questions to ask yourself.

- What activities make me lose track of time?

- When do I feel the most alive?

- What are my core values?

- What do I want people to remember me for?

Explore your passions and interests. List activities, subjects, or hobbies that excite you. Consider what you loved as a child or pursued in your free time.

Try new things. Step outside your comfort zone. Attend workshops, take classes, or volunteer in different areas to discover what resonates with you.

Ask for feedback from friends, family, or colleagues. Find out what they believe are your greatest strengths. Their perspectives can provide you with valuable insights.

Identify your values. Write down the principles that are most important to you (e.g., honesty, adventure, compassion). Which are non-negotiable and guide your decisions?

Imagine your ideal life by creating a vision board. Use images and words that represent your dreams and desires. Visualising your ideal life can clarify your purpose.

Imagine your legacy. Think about the impact you want to have on the world. What do you want to contribute?

Set goals and act by breaking down your purpose into actionable, achievable goals. Use the SMART (Specific, Measurable, Achievable, Relevant, Time-bound) criteria. Outline the steps needed to reach your goals. Stay flexible as you learn more about yourself along the way.

Seek inspiration from others. Connect with people who inspire you. Learn about how they discovered their own purposes.

Read books on personal development and purpose. Consider titles such as "Man's Search for Meaning" by Viktor Frankl or "The Purpose Driven Life" by Rick Warren.

Your purpose may evolve over time. Be open to new experiences and shifts in perspective. Engage in practices like meditation or yoga to help cultivate inner peace and clarity. Quieten your mind and pay attention to your intuition. Your inner self can provide valuable insights about your purpose.

Engaging with others and contributing to your community can provide a sense of belonging and purpose. Discuss your thoughts and experiences with trusted friends or support groups. Sometimes, talking can lead to deeper insights.

Discovering your life purpose is self-discovery that requires patience, courage, and persistence Take your time, and trust that with exploration, your purpose will reveal itself. Trust the process, follow your heart, and let your purpose guide you towards a fulfilling and meaningful life.

13. Be aware of your beliefs and values.

Core beliefs may have come from parents and teachers. Ask yourself if they are still valid or need to be discarded.

Your actions today may be ruled by beliefs from long ago. If there is something you want to do but find it difficult to take the vital first step ask yourself what's stopping you, what's the worst thing that could happen if you did that?

Discarding old beliefs and taking on new ones is sometimes the vital first step you need to take to get your life on a different track

Look within yourself and identify what really matters to you. To recognise your beliefs and values, the first step is introspection. What are your core principles and what do you stand for? Your beliefs and values stem from your upbringing, personal experiences, interactions with different people, and the choices you have made in life.

Notice what makes you happy, fulfilled, and satisfied. What motivates you to do the things you do, and what makes you feel proud of yourself? These are indicators of what holds value to you.

Try to understand why certain beliefs and values are important to you. What are the benefits of holding these beliefs and values, and what does it mean to let them guide your decisions and actions?

Recognising your beliefs and values is an essential step toward self-awareness and personal growth. Here's a guide to help you identify and understand what truly matters to you. Understanding the significance of your beliefs and values will help you to talk about them better and stay true to yourself.

Be open to change. As you continue to grow and experience life, your beliefs and values may evolve. Be willing to evaluate them and see if they still support with who you are and what you stand for. Take some time to think about significant experiences in your life. Consider moments that made you feel particularly proud, fulfilled, or even disappointed. Ask yourself:

- What was happening during those times?
- What emotions did I feel?
- What did I learn from these experiences?
- How did I react, and why?

Reflect on your beliefs, where they come from and whether you genuinely hold them or if they were inherited from others. Think about the individuals who have shaped your views and attitudes. This could include family members, friends, mentors, or even public figures.

- What qualities do you admire in them?
- What beliefs or values do they embody that resonate with you?
- How have they influenced your thinking or decisions?

Evaluate your reactions. Pay attention to how you respond to different situations, especially when faced with ethical dilemmas or conflicts.

- What emotions do I feel during these situations?
- What factors influence my decisions?
- Are there patterns in my responses that reveal my core beliefs?

Create a list of values that are important to you. You can start by reviewing a list of common values (like honesty, integrity, kindness, success, etc.) and select the ones that resonate with you. Narrow it down to your top five to ten values.

- Which values do you put first?
- Are there values that you are willing to defend?

Jot down your beliefs about various topics. This could include beliefs about:

- Relationships
- Success and failure
- Education
- Society and culture
- Politics

Seek feedback. Getting an outside perspective can be helpful. Consider discussing your beliefs and values with trusted friends or family members. Ask them questions like:

- How do you see my values reflected in my actions?
- Are there areas where you think my beliefs may not be reflected with my behaviour?

Journal your thoughts. Writing about your beliefs and values can help clarify them. Keep a journal where you explore your thoughts and feelings on a regular basis. Think about:

- Your current beliefs: Are they serving you well?
- Changes in your beliefs. Have they evolved over time?
- How your values affect your choices and life direction.

Revisit and revise. Understanding your beliefs and values is an ongoing process. As you experience life, you may find that your values and beliefs shift. Make it a habit to reassess them regularly.

Align your life with your values. Once you have a clear understanding of your beliefs and values, try to associate your actions and decisions with them. Ask yourself:

- Do your daily choices reflect your values?
- Are there any areas of your life that feel out of line?
- What changes can you make to ensure greater connection?

Recognising your beliefs and values is a journey that takes time, patience, and honesty. It can lead to greater self-awareness and fulfillment. It's perfectly normal for beliefs and values to evolve as you grow and experience life. Accepting change will help you to approach life with an open mindset and continue to learn and grow as a person.

14. Increase your skills.

Improving your skills can be something that enhances both your personal and professional life.

What do you need to learn? What do you already know? What transferable skills do you have? These may be in relation not only to your working life and professional skills but also skills you have in your domestic and social life. What would be useful when you move into the life you really want?

When and how will you go about acquiring new skills which you may need? Can you ever know it all? Don't wait until you are 'perfect'. Start as soon as possible. Learn as you go along and adapt to the new circumstances.

Lifelong learning is important to keep your brain active and to enable you to let your life experiences and learning mature. You are not too old to learn something new! It is important to continually increase your skills and competencies to stay relevant and competitive in your professional life.

Look for industry-specific training that can enhance your skills and knowledge. This way, you can keep up with the latest trends and developments in your field.

Take online courses. There are many available that offer training and certification for a variety of skills. You can take courses from your own home at your own pace.

Read work-related publications and stay up to date on the latest news and developments in your field. This will help you stay informed and aware of new technologies and changes within your industry.

Network with other professionals can be a great way to learn from others and stay informed about the latest trends and developments.

Volunteer for additional responsibilities at work to challenge yourself and learn new skills. This will also show your employer that you are proactive and willing to take on new challenges.

Identify skills to improve by reflecting on your current skills and identifying gaps or areas for improvement. Decide which skills you want to focus on. Consider both soft skills (communication, teamwork) and hard skills (technical, organisational). Update your skills as industries evolve, continuously seeking to update and refine your skills.

Create a learning plan with what resources you'll use, timelines, and targets. Include various methods such as online courses, workshops, books, and podcasts to keep your learning appealing. Find free, quality tutorials and instructional videos relevant to your skill area. Webinars and workshops offer the chance to participate in live sessions and interact with instructors.

Practise your skill, focusing on areas that challenge you. Set aside time each week to practise.

Find a mentor who can provide guidance, support, and feedback on your progress. Collaborate with colleagues or join study groups to exchange knowledge and receive constructive critiques.

Apply your skills by looking for opportunities to apply what you've learned in real-life scenarios, volunteer projects, or freelance work. Develop your own projects or challenges that utilise and showcase your skill. Join communities (online or offline) related to your skill area to find inspiration, support, and networking opportunities.

Track your progress by regularly assessing your improvement against your goals. Keep a journal to document your experiences, challenges, and breakthroughs. Recognise and celebrate small wins to stay motivated.

Improving your skills is continuous. it involves effort, practice, and a willingness to learn. You can improve your abilities, increase your confidence, and broaden your opportunities for personal and professional growth. Persistence is key, and every small step contributes to your overall progress.

15. Change one thing.

Have you ever used a spreadsheet to work out the effect of, for example, paying different amounts of money each month? Perhaps you want to invest to save for something in a certain period. By altering the amount saved, or the amount of interest earned each month you notice how all the totals change too.

When you change one thing, everything else changes, just like a spreadsheet.

Imagine a bustling city where everyone is stressed, on their way to work. Now, picture a single individual, who decides to start each day with a simple morning routine: she takes ten minutes to meditate before leaving her house.

At first, it seems insignificant, just a few moments of quiet in a noisy world. But this one change ripples throughout her day.

With her mind cleared and centred, she approaches her day differently. She is more present in her interactions, listening deeply to her colleagues and responding thoughtfully. This connection improves teamwork and creativity.

Energised by her calmness, she eats a nutritious breakfast instead of her usual rushed coffee and pastry. This leads her to have more energy, and as she becomes more aware of her health, she includes exercise into her routine.

When faced with obstacles at work, instead of reacting with frustration, she takes a deep breath and looks for solutions. Her problem-solving skills become sharper, improving her performance and boosting her confidence.

She begins including small breaks throughout her day for reflection and breathing exercises. This change helps her reduce stress, and she notices that her focus improves significantly, allowing her to accomplish tasks more efficiently.

Her positive changes don't go unnoticed. They encourage others. Colleagues are curious about her newfound energy and approach to work. They begin to ask questions and, inspired by her, start their own morning rituals. Some take walks, while others begin journalling.

Over time, these individual changes lead to a shift in workplace culture, to a more co-operative and supportive environment. Stress levels decrease, and productivity soars as the entire team finds joy in their work.

As her life changes, she starts exploring new hobbies and interests she never had time for before. She joins a local art class, spends time volunteering, and rekindles old friendships, each adding richness to her life that she had overlooked.

Her story highlights that changing one small thing—like taking a few moments for yourself, can set off an entire chain reaction in your life. It triggers a shift that can alter perspectives, improve well-being, and foster stronger connections. Sometimes, the smallest change can lead to the most profound transformations.

There is an interconnection between the parts of any system. Changing something in one area will influence other areas of your life. For example, if you don't know what to do about a job you hate, you will find that after tidying some cupboards and throwing away things you no longer need, seems to create some space for new things to come into your life.

Life is like a spreadsheet, a series of interconnected cells that require balance and organisation to function properly. Each cell represents a different aspect of life, such as work, relationships, health or hobbies, all of which have a direct impact on your overall well-being.

Similarly, in life, each day is like a new row, and every experience or incident that happens to us is like a new piece of data. Your success in life is determined by how well you manage the various aspects of your life. Just like a spreadsheet, your life needs to be organised into sections and given a clear direction.

You need to identify your priorities and goals, allocate the necessary resources (time, money, energy) to achieve them and regularly monitor your progress.

You also need to adjust to changes in your life. Just as data in a cell can be edited, deleted or added, you need to be flexible and adaptable to life's inevitable ups and downs. Sometimes you may need to make tough choices, and like a spreadsheet, you need to weigh the pros and cons before deciding.

Life, like a spreadsheet, presents a series of choices that require careful consideration, organisation, and management.

Your success in life directly relates to how you manage aspects of your life, and how you react to any changes that come your way.

Imagine if, instead of viewing challenges as obstacles, you approach them as opportunities for growth. Adopting a growth mindset, the belief that abilities and intelligence can be developed through dedication and hard work, could transform every aspect of your life.

Instead of feeling discouraged by setbacks or feedback, see them as valuable lessons that propel you forward. This shift could lead to seeking new opportunities, embracing learning, and ultimately achieving career milestones you once thought were out of reach.

Viewing conflicts in relationships as chances for understanding rather than threats could enhance communication and deepen connections.

This could lead to healthier, more supportive relationships with friends, family, and colleagues.

By adopting a positive mindset towards your physical and mental health, you focus on progress rather than perfection. You experiment with new habits, learn from slip-ups, and celebrate small victories, making it easier to lead a healthier lifestyle.

Embracing the idea that creativity can be stimulated rather than a fixed trait will encourage you to explore new hobbies and express yourself without the fear of judgment. This could lead to discovering untapped talents and passions.

A positive mindset fosters strength, enabling you to bounce back from failures with renewed determination. This change in perspective enables you to face life's challenges with hope and optimism.

In essence, changing your mindset can fundamentally alter the course of your life, affecting everything from career and relationships to health and creativity. It all starts with the choice to embrace a positive mindset.

Life, much like a spreadsheet, is made up of various components. Just as rows and columns group information, your life is filled with different parts: family, work, hobbies, and friends, each with their own place and importance.

Every experience adds a new piece of data. Some entries are straightforward and happy, such as a promotion at work, a joyful reunion, or a dream realised. Others might be messy or challenging, for example, loss, disappointment, or change. Each experience contributes to the overall picture of who you are.

Formulas for growth. Like formulas that calculate sums and averages, your choices and actions combine to create outcomes. The more you cherish your relationships and invest in personal growth, the greater the rewards.

Conditional formatting. Just as spreadsheets use colour to highlight key information, your emotions act as indicators in life. Joy, sadness, and stress signal when you need to pay attention to your wellbeing or make a change.

Sorting and filtering. Life can get overwhelming, much like a cluttered spreadsheet. Sometimes you need to sort your priorities and filter out the noise, focusing on what truly matters, whether it is goals, passions, or important relationships.

Errors and debugging. Errors are inevitable, just like faults in a formula. Life teaches you to identify and learn from these mistakes, leading to improvement. Sometimes you need to 'debug' your life, reevaluate your choices and make necessary adjustments.

Saving progress. Continuous learning and memory conservation are key. Just as you save your work, it's important to reflect on experiences, good or bad, so that you can build on them and move forward.

Spreadsheets stand out when shared. Similarly, life is enriched through collaboration and connection. Working together with others can lead to new insights, joint successes, and shared happiness.

A spreadsheet has endless potential for growth, just like you. With every new cell, you can enter new data, discover new paths, and craft a unique history that reflects your journey.

Life is like a spreadsheet, an intricate, multi-dimensional creation where every entry contributes to the overall story. Embrace the process, learn from each cell, and remember you have the power to edit, to change, and to thrive!

16. Do what you must do.

Life is filled with moments that challenge you, push your limits, and demand action. When faced with a decision, a task, or a necessary change, it's essential to remember one key thing: 'Now do what you must do'.

Half full or half empty? The secret for change is positive thinking. Become aware of your thoughts and notice how often you assume something can't happen or that you personally wouldn't be able to do something.

Start to rephrase your negative words into positive statements. These become your affirmations, which state something as if it is already happening.

Take a moment to assess where you are and what needs to be addressed. Accept the challenges, but don't let them stop you.

Identify what is most important.

- What requires your immediate attention?
- What can wait?

Organising your tasks can provide clarity and make the workload seem less daunting.

Take a deep breath. Sometimes, all it takes is a moment to gather your thoughts. Inhale deeply, exhale slowly, and centre yourself before taking the next step.

Break it down. Large tasks can be overwhelming. Decide what are manageable steps. Focus on one small action at a time.

Commit to action. Once you've planned, it's time to act. Whether it's making a phone call, sending an email, or taking a step towards a goal, commit to making that move now.

Concentrate. Distractions are inevitable, but it's important to stay focused on the task at hand. Eliminate or minimise distractions to maximise results.

Reflect and adjust, as you move through your tasks. Take a moment to reflect. Is what you're doing effective? If not, don't hesitate to adjust your approach.

Celebrate progress, no matter how small, celebrate your achievements along the way. Recognising progress can motivate you to keep moving forward.

Keep moving forward, even if the path isn't clear, take the next step. Every action, no matter how small, is a step toward reaching your goals.

Stay committed. Sometimes, the hardest part is simply sticking with it. Remind yourself of your purpose and why you're doing what you must do.

Now, do what you must do. Your future depends on the choices you make today.

Don't miss out!

Visit the website below and you can sign up to receive emails whenever Susan Kersley publishes a new book. There's no charge and no obligation.

https://books2read.com/r/B-A-EFNC-IURDF

BOOKS2READ

Connecting independent readers to independent writers.

Did you love *16 Ways to Change Your Life*? Then you should read *How to Have a Balanced Life*[1] by Susan Kersley!

[2]

Chaotic life? Never get much done? Want more balance?

Simple changes can give you big results.

Are you neglecting important aspects of your life because you don't have enough balance? Do you struggle to achieve what you want?

Let Susan Kersley guide you through simple steps to reach your goals, find more balance and rediscover forgotten parts of yourself.

The author is a retired medical doctor and was a life coach for fifteen years.

How to have a balanced life is a well written, concise personal development book with easy to follow suggestions that will make a big

---

1. https://books2read.com/u/brlLzm

2. https://books2read.com/u/brlLzm

difference to your life. You'll find simple changes you can make today and discover how these will have a rapid positive impact on your life.

Buy the book today and find your way to peace and personal stability.

Read more at https://susankersley.co.uk.

Also by Susan Kersley

A Novel
Pills and Pillboxes
Connection Deception

Books about Weight Management
Change Your Mind, Change Your Weight
Weight Loss Success
Mind Over Weight

Books for Doctors
ABC of Change for Doctors
Life After Medicine
Prescription for Change
Lifestyle Coaching for Doctors
The Busy Doctor's Guide: Improve your Work-Life Balance
Work-Life Balance for Doctors
Simple Ways to Meet the Challenges of Working as a Doctor
Meet the Challenges of Working as a Doctor

About the Author

Susan Kersley has written personal development and self-help books for doctors and others, and books about retirement and novels.

She was a doctor for thirty years and then left Medicine to be a Life Coach..

Now retired, she is updating her books and writing more. Please visit her website https://susankersley.co.uk

If you enjoyed this book, **please take a moment to leave a review.** Reviews are so important for independent authors.

Read more at https://susankersley.co.uk.

www.ingramcontent.com/pod-product-compliance
Lightning Source LLC
Chambersburg PA
CBHW020330180726
47991CB00019B/1127